Christmas:

Reflections on the Joy of the Season

Edited by Heather Russell-Revesz

BARNES & NOBLE BOOKS

NEW YORK

For Joe.

The quotes in this book have been drawn from many sources, and are assumed to be accurate as quoted in their previously published forms. Although every effort has been made to verify the quotes and sources, the publisher cannot guarantee their perfect accuracy.

Compilation copyright © 2003 by Barnes & Noble, Inc.

2003 Barnes & Noble Books

ISBN 0-7607-4058-5

Printed and bound in the United States of America

M 9 8 7 6 5 4 3 2

MY MOM LOVES DECORATING HER HOUSE FOR Christmas. It always looks picture perfect— from the tinsel placed ever so delicately on the huge Douglas fir, to the ribbons intertwined with pine boughs on the fireplace mantle. Even the guest bedroom gets little stuffed elves (Jingle and Jangle) and a scented gingerbread candle. This knack for holiday decorating (I call it the "Xmasome") was passed on to both my sisters, whose houses in December give Martha Stewart's a run for her money. Somehow it has even rubbed off on my sister-in-law, who not only sets a mean holiday table but also makes her own cranberry sauce. From scratch.

But not me.

The Xmasome passed me by. I think about decorating. I think about making cookies and a gingerbread house and dressing up my cat in a Santa hat…but somehow it just never happens.

Thankfully, my Mom did pass along to me a love for Christmas and what it stands for, not just what it looks like. For as fabulous as my Mom's house always looks, she never ever loses sight of the fact that Christmas is about family, love, and sharing. I learned from her that Christmas is the time to open your heart, think of others, and give thanks for all the blessings in your life.

I hope *Christmas: Reflections on the Joy of the Season* will help you recall fond memories of Christmases past, and add a touch of warmth and fun to your holiday season. You may even be inspired to trim your tree like it has never been done before. And this may just be the year I break out the garland and mistletoe for my own house...

Happy Holidays!
Heather Russell-Revesz

Christmas Is...

Christmas, children, is not a date. It is a state of mind.

—MARY ELLEN CHASE, educator

Christmas is the season for kindling the fire of hospitality in the hall, the genial flame of charity in the heart.

—WASHINGTON IRVING

A good conscience is a continual Christmas.

—BENJAMIN FRANKLIN

What is Christmas? It is tenderness for the past, courage for the present, hope for the future. It is a fervent wish that every cup may overflow with blessings rich and eternal, and that every path may lead to peace.

—AGNES M. PHARO

We consider Christmas as the encounter, the great encounter, the historical encounter, the decisive encounter, between God and mankind. He who has faith knows this truly; let him rejoice.

—POPE PAUL VI, 1965 Christmas address

There has been only one Christmas—the rest are anniversaries.

—W. J. CAMERON, author

I believe that the eternal lesson of Christmas is to inspire us to use our God-given gifts to build a better world.

—Norman Vincent Peale

I am not alone at all, I thought. I was never alone at all. And that, of course, is the message of Christmas. We are never alone. Not when the night is darkest, the wind coldest, the word seemingly most indifferent. For this is still the time God chooses.

—Taylor Caldwell, "My Christmas Miracle"

Christmas is the day that holds time together.

—Alexander Smith, poet

Christmas is the gentlest, loveliest festival of the revolving year—and yet, for all that, when it speaks, its voice has strong authority.

—W. J. CAMERON, author

The earth has grown old with its burden of care,
But at Christmas it always is young.

—PHILLIPS BROOKS, Episcopal bishop

There are no strangers on Christmas Eve.

—MICHAEL O'BRIEN, *Beyond Tomorrow*, 1940

Christmas, my child, is always.

—DALE EVANS

The Birth

Good news from heaven the angels bring,
Glad tidings to the earth they sing:
To us this day a child is given,
To crown us with the joy of heaven.

—MARTIN LUTHER

Awake, glad heart! Get up and sing,
It is the birthday of thy King.

—HENRY VAUGHAN, "Christ's Nativity"

And she brought forth her firstborn son, and
wrapped him in swaddling clothes, and laid
him in a manger; because there was no room
for them in the inn.

And there were in the same country shepherds
abiding in the field, keeping watch over their
flock by night.

And, lo, the angel of the Lord came upon them,
and the glory of the Lord shone round about
them; and they were sore afraid.

And the angel said unto them, Fear not: for,
behold, I bring you good tidings of great joy,
which shall be to all people.

For unto you is born this day in the city of
David a Saviour, which is Christ the Lord.

And this *shall be* a sign unto you; Ye shall find
the babe wrapped in swaddling clothes,
lying in a manger.

And suddenly there was with the angel a
multitude of the heavenly host praising God,
and saying,

Glory to God in the highest, and on earth
peace, goodwill toward men.

—LUKE 2:7-14

And she will bear a Son, and you shall
call His name Jesus, for it is He who
will save His people from their sins.

—Matthew 1:21

A barn shall harbour heaven,
A stall become a shrine.

—Richard Wilbur, "A Christmas Hymn"

I sing the birth was born tonight,
The Author both of life and light;
The angels so did sound it,
And like the ravished shepherds said,
Who saw the light, and were afraid,
Yet searched, and true they found it.

—Ben Jonson,
"A Hymn on the Nativity of My Savior"

Fall on your knees
O hear the angel voices
O night divine
O night when Christ was born.

—ADOLPHE ADAM, "O Holy Night"

Christmas in Bethlehem. The ancient dream: a cold, clear night made brilliant by a glorious star, the smell of incense, shepherds and wise men falling to their knees in adoration of the sweet baby, the incarnation of perfect love.

—LUCINDA FRANKS, "Pilgrimage"

God rest ye merry, gentlemen,
Let nothing you dismay,
Remember Christ our Savior,
Was born on Christmas Day;
To save us all from Satan's pow'r,
When we were gone astray
O tidings of comfort and joy . . .

—TRADITIONAL ENGLISH CAROL,
"God Rest Ye Merry Gentlemen"

Shall I tell you who will come
to Bethlehem on Christmas Morn,
Who will kneel them gently down
before the Lord, new-born?

—TRADITIONAL SPANISH CAROL

The feet of the humblest may walk
    in the field
Where the feet of the Holiest trod,
This, then, is the marvel
    to mortals revealed.

—PHILLIPS BROOKS, Episcopal bishop

This is the month, and this the happy morn,
Wherein the Son of Heav'n's Eternal King,
Of wedded Maid, and Virgin Mother born,
Our great redemption from above did bring.

—JOHN MILTON,
"On the Morning of Christ's Nativity"

Men may come and men may go
But none will
ever find a way
To banish Christ
from Christmas Day...

—HELEN STEINER RICE, "The Miracle of Christmas"

O Christmas Sun! What holy task is thine!
To fold a world in the embrace of God!

—GUY WETMORE CARRYL, poet

It was poor little Jesus,
Yes, yes
He was born on Christmas,
Yes, yes
And laid in a manger,
Yes, yes.

—AFRICAN AMERICAN SPIRITUAL

The time draws near the birth of Christ,
The moon is hid—the night is still;
The Christmas bells from hill to hill
Answer each other in the mist.

—Lord Alfred Tennyson, "The Birth of Christ"

And is it true? And is it true,
This most tremendous tale of all,
Seen in a stained-glass window's hue,
A Baby in an in ox's stall?
The Maker of the stars and sea
Became a Child on earth for me?

—Sir John Betjeman, "Christmas"

This is Christmas: not the tinsel, not the giving and receiving, not even the carols, but the humble heart that receives anew the wondrous gift, the Christ.

—Frank McKibben

The Christ-child lay on Mary's lap,
His hair was like a light.
(O weary, weary was the world,
But here is all aright.)

The Christ-child stood at Mary's knee,
His hair was like a crown,
And all the flowers looked up at Him
And all the stars looked down.

—G. K. CHESTERTON, "The Christ-child"

Some say that ever 'gainst that season comes
Wherein our Saviour's birth is celebrated,
The bird of dawning singeth all night long;
And then, they say, no spirit can walk abroad;
The nights are wholesome; then no planets strike,
No fairy takes, nor witch hath power to charm,
So hallow'd and so gracious is the time.

—WILLIAM SHAKESPEARE, *Hamlet*

Loving Father, help us remember the birth of
    Jesus, that we may share in the song of the
    angels, the gladness of the shepherds, and
    the worship of the wise men.

Close the door of hate and open the door of love
    all over the world.

Let kindness come with every gift and good
    desires with every greeting.

Deliver us from evil by the blessing which Christ
    brings, and teach us to be merry with clear
    hearts.

May the Christmas morning make us happy to
    be thy children,

and the Christmas evening bring us to our beds
    with grateful thoughts,

forgiving and forgiven, for Jesus' sake.

Amen!

—ROBERT LOUIS STEVENSON, "A Christmas Prayer"

How many observe Christ's birthday! How few, his precepts! O! 'tis easier to keep holidays than commandments.

—Benjamin Franklin

Love

Blessed is the season which engages the whole world in a conspiracy of love.

> —HAMILTON WRIGHT MABIE, writer

Every time we love, every time we give, it's Christmas.

> —DALE EVANS

If there is no joyous way to give a festive gift, give love away.

> —ANONYMOUS

15

Are you willing to believe that love is the strongest thing in the world—stronger than hate, stronger than evil, stronger than death—and that the blessed life which began in Bethlehem nineteen hundred years ago is the image and brightness of the Eternal Love? Then you can keep Christmas.

—HENRY VAN DYKE, poet

The Christmas spirit—love—changes hearts and lives.

—PAT BOONE

Christmas is most truly Christmas when we celebrate it by giving the light of love to those who need it most.

—RUTH CARTER STAPLETON

Three times my shadow crossed your floor,
Three times I came to your lowly door;
For I was the beggar with bruised cold feet;
I was the woman you gave something to eat;
And I was the child on the homeless street.
Three times I knocked, three times I came in,
And each time I found the warmth of a friend.
Of all the gifts, love is the best;
I was honored to be your Christmas Guest.

> —EDWIN MARKHAM, "The Christmas Guest"

Remember
This December,
That love weighs more than gold!

> —JOSEPHINE DODGE DASKAM BACON, playwright

Just write "love" on the Christmas tags;
That's what I want for Christmas.

> —IRVING CAESAR, songwriter

Best of all, Christmas means a spirit of love, a time when the love of God and the love of our fellow men should prevail over all hatred and bitterness, a time when our thoughts and deeds and the spirit of our lives manifest the presence of God.

—GEORGE F. McDOUGALL, reverend

The only real blind person at Christmastime is he who has not Christmas in his heart.

—HELEN KELLER

It's the most wonderful present I ever had. There's nothing so wonderful as sense—except love.

—ELIZABETH MORROW, *A Pint of Judgement*

See Him in a manger laid,
Whom the choirs of angels praise;
Mary, Joseph, lend your aid,
While our hearts in love we raise.

—TRADITIONAL HYMN,
"Angels We Have Heard on High"

After all, if we cannot hear the carol and see the heavenly messenger, it is because our ears are deaf and our eyes are blind, not that we turn willfully away from love or beauty.

—WILLA CATHER

Love came down at Christmas,
Love all lovely, Love Divine;
Love was born at Christmas;
Star and angels gave the sign.

—CHRISTINA ROSSETTI

A Savior King was born that day,
A baby just like you,
And as the Magi came with gifts,
I come with my gift too

That peace on earth fills up your time,
That brotherhood surrounds you.
That you may know the warmth of love,
And wrap it all around you.

—JOHN DENVER, "A Baby Just Like You"

I will honor Christmas in my heart, and try to keep it all the year.

—CHARLES DICKENS

Peace

I heard the bells, on Christmas Day
Their old, familiar carols play,
And wild and sweet
The words repeat
Of peace on earth, good will to men!

—HENRY WADSWORTH LONGFELLOW

A very merry Christmas
And a happy New Year
Let's hope it's a good one
Without any fear.

—JOHN LENNON, "Happy Christmas (War Is Over)"

Peace is always beautiful.

—WALT WHITMAN

Peace on earth, goodwill to men
From heaven's all gracious King.

—EDMUND H. SEARS,
"It Came Upon the Midnight Clear"

On this Christmas, may we, the people of every race, nation, and religion, learn to love one another and to forgive and be forgiven. Then the peace of Christ will prevail.

—CORETTA SCOTT KING

If all mamas and daddies was sittin' back safe and secure in the knowledge that they'd have toys and goodies for their children…that would bring on a little more peace.

—ALICE CHILDRESS, "Merry Christmas, Marge!"

As fits the holy Christmas birth,
Be this, good friends, our carol still—
Be peace on earth, be peace on earth,
To men of gentle will.

—WILLIAM MAKEPEACE THACKERAY

Bless us Lord, this Christmas, with quietness
    of mind;
Teach us to be patient and always to be kind.

—HELEN STEINER RICE

Peace! Peace! Jesus Christ was born to save.

—TRADITIONAL GERMAN CAROL,
"Good Christian Men, Rejoice"

Christmas waves a magic wand over this world, and
behold, everything is softer and more beautiful.

—NORMAN VINCENT PEALE

Peace on earth, and mercy mild, God and sinners reconciled.

—CHARLES WESLEY, "Hark! The Herald Angels Sing"

Peace on earth will come to stay, when we live Christmas every day.

—HELEN STEINER RICE

Joy

Joy to the world! The Lord is come:
Let earth receive her King.
Let ev'ry heart prepare him room,
And heaven and nature sing.

—Isaac Watts, "Joy to the World"

From home to home, and heart to heart, from one
place to another. The warmth and joy of Christmas,
brings us closer to each other.

—Emily Matthews, poet

Somehow, not only for Christmas
But all the long year through,
The joy that you give to others
Is the joy that comes back to you.
And the more you spend in blessing
The poor and lonely and sad,
The more of your heart's possessing
Returns to you glad.

—John Greenleaf Whittier, "The Joy of Giving"

The joy of brightening other lives, bearing each others' burdens, easing others' loads and supplanting empty hearts and lives with generous gifts becomes for us the magic of Christmas.

—W. C. Jones, author

Joy is the serious business of heaven.

—C. S. Lewis

Villagers all, this frosty tide,
Let your doors swing open wide,
Though wind may follow, and snow beside,
Yet draw us in by your fire to bide;
Joy shall be yours in the morning!

—KENNETH GRAHAME, *The Wind in the Willows*

Have a holly, jolly Christmas;
It's the best time of the year
I don't know if there'll be snow,
but have a cup of cheer.

—JOHNNY MARKS, "Holly Jolly Christmas"

Loved ones, filled with lazy satisfaction following
　　the holiday dinner, surround the hearth . . .
Joy!
And most joyous of all . . . He is with us.

—JACK HAYFORD, "Joy!"

O how joyfully, O how merrily
Christmas comes with its grace divine!

—TRADITIONAL SICILIAN HYMN, "O, How Joyfully"

Everywhere, everywhere, Christmas tonight!

—PHILLIPS BROOKS, Episcopal bishop

Giving

The magi, as you know, were wise men—wonderfully wise men—who brought gifts to the Babe in the manger. They invented the art of giving Christmas presents.

—O. HENRY, "The Gift of the Magi"

Do give books—religious or otherwise—for Christmas. They're never fattening, seldom sinful, and permanently personal.

—LENORE HERSHEY

I always believed that the true spirit of Christmas demands thought and effort on the giver's part, not just lavish spending.

—INEZ HOGAN, writer

What can I give him,
Poor as I am?
If I were a shepherd
I would bring a lamb;
If I were a wise man
I would do my part;
Yet what I can I give him—
Give him my heart.

—CHRISTINA ROSSETTI, "In the Bleak Mid-winter"

A Christmas candle is a lovely thing; It makes no noise at all, But softly gives itself away; While quite unselfish, it grows small.

—EVA K. LOGUE

We three kings of Orient are;
Bearing gifts we traverse afar,
Field and fountain, moor and mountain,
Following yonder star.

–John H. Hopkins Jr.,
"We Three Kings of Orient Are"

The true spirit of Christmas calls for gifts, but for thoughtful gifts, not necessarily expensive gifts.

–Lionel Barrymore

We cannot give in the true Christmas spirit if we do not give to those who cannot afford to give anything in return.

–Clare Booth Luce

But when the real presents were discovered, the presents that meant no end of thought and management and secret self-denial, the brightest part of the household love and happiness shone out.

—SARA ORNE JEWETT, "Mrs. Perkins' Christmas Eve"

Giving presents is a talent; to know what a person wants, to know when and how to get it, to give it lovingly and well.

—PAMELA GLENCONNER

Therefore, Christian men, be sure,
Wealth or rank possessing,
Ye who now will bless the poor,
Shall yourselves find blessing.

—JOHN MASON NEALE, "Good King Wenceslas"

I have always thought of Christmastime as a good time; a kind, forgiving, charitable, pleasant time; the only time I know of, in the long calendar of the year, when men and women seem by one consent to open their shut-up hearts freely.

—CHARLES DICKENS

But in a last word to the wise of these days let it be said that of all who give gifts these two were the wisest. Of all who give and receive gifts, such as they are wisest. They are the magi.

—O. HENRY, "The Gift of the Magi"

The best of all gifts around any Christmas tree: the presence of a happy family all wrapped up in each other.

—BURTON HILLIS, *Better Homes and Gardens*

Were it not for the shepherds, there would have been no reception. And were it not for a group of stargazers, there would have been no gifts.

—MAX LUCADO, *God Came Near*

Christmas is a time for giving,
The Wise Men brought their best,
But Christ showed that the gift of self
Will out-give all the rest.

—FRED BAUER, "Time for Christmas"

The only gift is a portion of thyself.

—RALPH WALDO EMERSON

Thanks be to God for his indescribable gift!

—2 CORINTHIANS 9:15

Let us remember that the Christmas heart is a giving heart, a wide open heart that thinks of others first. The birth of the Baby Jesus stands as the most significant event in all history, because it has meant the pouring into a sick world of the healing medicine of love, which has transformed all manner of hearts for almost two thousand years... Underneath all the bulging bundles is this beating Christmas heart.

—GEORGE MATTHEW ADAMS, author

Santa

No Santa Claus! Thank God! he lives, and he lives forever. A thousand years from now, Virginia, nay, ten times ten thousand years from now, he will continue to make glad the heart of childhood.

—Francis P. Church

'Twas the night before Christmas, when all
    through the house
Not a creature was stirring, not even a mouse:
The stockings were hung by the chimney with
    care,
In hopes that St. Nicholas soon would be there.

—Clement Clarke Moore

Santy Claus, Santy Claus, listen to my plea,
I don't want nothin' for Christmas but my baby
back to me.

—"Santa Claus Blues"

"That's where I reckon Santa Claus comes in
To be our parents' pseudonymity
In Christmas giving, so they can escape
The thanks and let him catch it as a
    scapegoat..."

—ROBERT FROST, "From Plane to Plane"

Then when I say "Good-bye and merry Christmas
to my little Susie Clemens," you must say
"Good-bye, good old Santa Claus, I thank you
very much..."

—MARK TWAIN, "Susie's Letter from Santa"

Truly our Claus had wisdom, for his good fortune but strengthened his resolve to befriend the little ones of his own race... The youngsters soon came to know his merry, laughing face and the kind glance of his bright eyes; and the parents, while they regarded the young man with some scorn for loving children more than their elders, were content that the girls and boys had found a playfellow who seemed willing to amuse them.

—L. Frank Baum, "How Claus Made the First Toy"

Oh, what a laugh it would have been
If Daddy had only seen
Mommy kissing Santa Claus last night.

—T. Connor, "I Saw Mommy Kissing Santa Claus"

There've been over four hundred documented sightings of Santa Claus. Scientifically documented. And it's on the Internet, so you know it's true.

—Manny, from the television show *Monk*

When their parents suggested to the girls that Santa Claus might not be able to make it that year, they did not at first believe it possible that this could happen. It took time for them to accustom themselves to the idea that there could be winters too severe for even a saint who lived at the North Pole to travel through, and to accept the uncertainty of what they had supposed the most certain thing in life. It was an acceptance that did not come easy.

—OLIVER LA FARGE, "The Snow Too Deep"

He's making a list,
And checking it twice;
Gonna find out who's naughty and nice.
Santa Claus is coming to town.

—J. FRED COOTS AND HENRY GILLESPIE,
"Santa Claus is Coming to Town"

Bells are ringing, children singing;
All is merry and bright.
Hang your stockings and say your prayers,
'Cause Santa Claus comes tonight.

—GENE AUTRY AND OAKLEY HALDEMAN,
"Here Comes Santa Claus"

Jolly old Saint Nicholas,
Lean your ear this way;
Don't you tell a single soul,
What I'm going to say
Christmas Eve is coming soon;
Now you dear old man,
Whisper what you'll bring to me,
Tell me if you can.

—TRADITIONAL ENGLISH CAROL,
"Jolly Old Saint Nicholas,"

If you're really Santa Claus, you can get it for me.
And if you can't, you're only a nice man with a
white beard, like Mother said.

—SUSAN WALKER, in *Miracle on 34th Street*, 1947

Jennifer Bofinger, media spokeswoman for the
animal rights group People for the Ethical
Treatment of Animals, said despite the shabby
treatment of deer in general, her organization has
not received any complaints about how Santa
Claus treats his reindeer.

—ANONYMOUS, *The Los Angeles Times*

Grandma got run over by a reindeer.
Walking home from our house Christmas Eve.
You can say there's no such thing as Santa,
But as for me and Grandpa, we believe.

—DR. ELMO, "Grandma Got Run Over By a Reindeer"

I stopped believing in Santa Claus when I was six. Mother took me to see him in a department store, and he asked for my autograph.

—SHIRLEY TEMPLE BLACK

Wait a minute, you! I heard about people like you! Are you saying you don't believe in Santa Claus?! And you call yourselves superheroes?!

—THE TICK, from the cartoon *The Tick*

Merry

Heap on the wood!—the wind is chill;
But let it whistle as it will,
We'll keep our Christmas merry still.

—Sir Walter Scott

My merrie, merrie boyes,
The Christmas Log to the firing.

—Robert Herrick

While angels sing with pious mirth,
A glad New Year to all the earth.

—Martin Luther, "A Prayer"

At Christmas be merry,
And thankful withal,
And feast thy poor neighbors,
The great with the small.

—THOMAS TUSSER

Deck the hall with boughs of holly...
'Tis the season to be jolly.

—TRADITIONAL WELSH CAROL, "Deck the Halls"

Sing we all merrily
Christmas is here,
The day we love best
Of days in the year

—TRADITIONAL

We wish you a merry Christmas and a happy New Year.

—TRADITIONAL ENGLISH CAROL,
"We Wish You a Merry Christmas"

'Twas Christmas broach'd the mightiest ale;
'Twas Christmas told the merriest tale;
A Christmas gambol oft could cheer
The poor man's heart through half the year.

—SIR WALTER SCOTT

Happy, happy Christmas, that can win us back to the delusions of our childish days; that can recall to the old man the pleasures of his youth; that can transport the sailor and the traveler, thousands of miles away, back to his own fireside and his quiet home!

—CHARLES DICKENS, *The Pickwick Papers*

At Christmas play and make good cheer,
For Christmas comes but once a year.

—THOMAS TUSSER, *The Farmer's Daily Diet*

Through the years we all will be together
If the Fates allow
Hang a shining star upon the highest bough.
And have yourself a merry little Christmas now.

—HUGH MARTIN AND RALPH BLANE,
"Have Yourself a Merry Little Christmas"

Trimmings

O Christmas tree, O Christmas tree,
Much pleasure doth thou bring me!
For every year the Christmas tree,
Brings to us all both joy and glee.
O Christmas tree, O Christmas tree,
Much pleasure doth thou bring me!

—TRADITIONAL GERMAN CAROL, "O Christmas Tree"

It was brilliantly lighted by a multitude of little tapers; and everywhere sparkled and glittered with bright objects.

—CHARLES DICKENS, "A Christmas Tree"

I still have my Christmas tree. I looked at it today.
Sure enough, I couldn't see any forests.

—STEPHEN WRIGHT

He asked if I would sell my Christmas trees;
My woods—the young fir balsams like a place
Where houses all are churches and have spires.
I hadn't thought of them as Christmas trees...

—ROBERT FROST, "Christmas Trees"

Christmas is here:
Winds whistle shrill,
Icy and chill.
Little care we;
Little we fear
Weather without,
Sheltered about
The Mahogany Tree.

—WILLIAM MAKEPEACE THACKERAY,
"The Mahogany Tree"

The Christmas tree—which was twice as tall as Father—was covered with gold and silver apples... and nestled in the hollows of the spreading branches sat hundreds of tiny candles that twinkled like stars, showing off the candy blossoms and fruit with a warm, flickering glow.

—E. T. A. HOFFMAN, *The Nutcracker*

Now gay trees rise
Before your eyes,
Abloom with tempting cheer;
Blithe voices sing,
And blithe bells ring
For Christmastide is here.

—TRADITIONAL ENGLISH CAROL

They lighted the candles on the Christmas tree, and the young people capered about and were brimming over with secrets and shouted with delight, and the tree shown and glistened brave in its gay trimmings of walnuts covered with gold and silver paper, and little bags sewed with bright worsteds, and all sorts of pretty homemade trifles.

—Sara Orne Jewett, "Mrs. Perkins' Christmas Eve"

Rocking around the Christmas tree
at the Christmas party hop
Mistletoe hung where you can see
Every couple tries to stop.

—Johnny Marks,
"Rocking Around the Christmas Tree"

On one branch they hung little nets, cut out of colored paper; every net was filled with sweetmeats; golden apples and walnuts hung down, as if they grew there, and more than a hundred little candles, red, white, and blue, were fastened to the different boughs…and high on the summit of the Tree was fixed a tinsel star. It was splendid, particularly splendid.

—HANS CHRISTIAN ANDERSON, "The Fir Tree"

Gather around the Christmas tree!
Every bough has a burden now,
They are gifts of love for us, we trow;
For Christ is born, His love to show,
And give good gifts to men below.

—JOHN H. HOPKINS, JR.,
"Gather Around the Christmas Tree"

Before the ice is in the pools,
Before the skaters go,
Or any cheek at nightfall
Is tarnished by the snow,
Before the fields have finished,
Before the Christmas tree,
Wonder upon wonder
Will arrive to me!

—EMILY DICKINSON

Decorations of red
on a green Christmas tree
Won't mean a thing if
you're not here with me.

—B. HAYES AND J. JOHNSON, "Blue Christmas"

No one loves a Christmas tree on January 1.

—ERMA BOMBECK

Feasting

So now is come our joyful feast;
Let every man be jolly.
Each room with ivy leaves is dressed
And every post with holly.
Though some churls at our mirth repine,
Round your foreheads garlands twine,
Drown sorrow in a cup of wine,
And let us all be merry.

—GEORGE WITHER, poet

A three-year-old gave this reaction to her Christmas dinner: "I don't like the turkey, but I like the bread he ate."

—ANONYMOUS

Little Jack Horner
Sat in the corner,
Eating a Christmas pie;
He put in his thumb,
And pulled out a plum,
And said, What a good boy am I!

—MOTHER GOOSE

There never was such a Christmas dinner as they had that day. The fat turkey was a sight to behold, when Hannah served him up, stuffed, browned, and decorated; so was the plum pudding, which quite melted in one's mouth; likewise the jellies, in which Amy reveled like a fly in a honey pot.

—LOUISA MAY ALCOTT, *Little Women*

Heaped on the floor, to form a kind of throne, were turkeys, geese, game, great joints of meat, long wreaths of sausages, mince pies, plum puddings, barrels of oysters, red-hot chestnuts, cherry-cheeked apples, juicy oranges, and immense cakes.

—CHARLES DICKENS, *A Christmas Carol*

Now that the time has come wherein
Our Savior Christ was born,
The larder's full of beef and pork,
The granary's full of corn.
As God hath plenty to thee sent,
Take comfort of thy labors,
And let it never thee repent,
To feast thy needy neighbors.

—POOR RICHARD'S ALMANAC

If a man turn sulky and drink by himself at Christmastime, he may make up his mind to be not a bit the better for it.

—CHARLES DICKENS,
"The Story of the Goblins Who Stole a Sexton"

She saw a table spread with a damask cloth and set with the finest porcelain. In the center, on a dish, lay a roasted goose stuffed with apples and prunes!

—HANS CHRISTIAN ANDERSON,
"The Little Match Girl"

Everybody knows
A turkey
and some mistletoe
Help to make the season bright.

—MEL TORME, "The Christmas Song"

The heavenly aroma still hung heavy in the house, but it was gone, all gone! No turkey! No turkey sandwiches, no turkey salad, no turkey gravy, turkey hash, turkey a la king, or gallons of turkey soup! Gone, all gone!

—RALPHIE, from *A Christmas Story*, 1983

Memories

Time was with most of us, when Christmas Day, encircling all our limited world like a magic ring, left nothing out for us to miss or seek; bound together all our home enjoyments, affections, and hopes; grouped everything and everyone round the Christmas fire, and made the little picture shining in our bright young eyes, complete.

—CHARLES DICKENS

Our hearts grow tender with childhood memories and love of kindred, and we are better throughout the year for having, in spirit, become a child again at Christmastime.

—LAURA INGALLS WILDER

61

The merry family gatherings—
The old, the very young;
The strangely lovely way they
Harmonize in carols sung.

For Christmas is tradition time—
Traditions that recall
The precious memories down the years,
The sameness of them all.

—HELEN LOWRIE MARSHALL, poet

It comes every year and will go on forever. And along with Christmas belong the keepsakes and the customs. Those humble, everyday things a mother clings to, and ponders, like Mary in the secret spaces of her heart.

—MARJORIE HOLMES

grandmama
sewing a new
button on my last year
ragdoll.

—CAROL FREEMAN, "Christmas Morning"

Here were kept up the old games of hoodman blind, shoe the wild mare, hot cockles, steal the white loaf, bob apple, and snapdragon: the Yule-log and Christmas candle were regularly burnt, and the mistletoe, with its white berries, hung up to the imminent peril of the housemaids.

—WASHINGTON IRVING

The song "White Christmas" is like an old Christmas memory: It inspires a happy sadness in the heart.

—BING CROSBY

My children teased me because their stockings inevitably contained toothbrushes, toothpaste, nail cleaners, soap, washcloths, etc. They said Mother never ceased to remind them that cleanliness was next to godliness—even on Christmas morning.

—ELEANOR ROOSEVELT, "Christmas at Hyde Park"

The wind bit hard at Valley Forge one Christmas.
Soldiers tied rags on their feet.
Red footprints wrote on the snow

—CARL SANDBURG,
"Washington Monument by Night"

The rooms were very still while the pages were softly turned and the winter sunshine crept in to touch the bright heads and serious faces with a Christmas greeting.

—LOUISA MAY ALCOTT

Should auld acquaintance be forgot
And never brought to mind?
Should auld acquaintance be forgot
And days of auld lang syne?

—ROBERT BURNS, "Auld Lang Syne"

There's a little vanity chair that Charlie gave me
the first Christmas we knew each other. I'll not be
parting with that, nor our bed—the four-poster—
I'll be needing that to die in.

—HELEN HAYES

How grand it feels to click your heels
And join in the fun of the jigs and reels
I'm handing you no blarney
The likes you've never known
Is Christmas in Killarney
With all of the folks at home.

—TRADITIONAL IRISH SONG, "Christmas in Killarney"

There is no ideal Christmas; only the one Christmas you decide to make as a reflection of your values, desires, affections, traditions.

—BILL McKIBBEN, *Hundred Dollar Holiday*

When Christmas bells are swinging above the
    fields of snow,
We hear sweet voices ringing from lands of
    long ago,
        And etched on vacant places
        Are half forgotten faces
Of friends we used to cherish, and loves we
    used to know—
When Christmas bells are swinging above the
    fields of snow.

—ELLA WHEELER WILCOX, "Christmas Fancies"

Christmas—that magic blanket that wraps itself about us, that something so intangible that it is like a fragrance. It may weave a spell of nostalgia. Christmas may be a day of feasting, or of prayer, but always it will be a day of remembrance—a day in which we think of everything we have ever loved.

—Augusta E. Rundel

Bah Humbug!

"Bah!" said Scrooge, "Humbug!... If I could work my will...every idiot who goes about with 'Merry Christmas' on his lips, should be boiled with his own pudding, and buried with a stake of holly through his heart."

—CHARLES DICKENS, *A Christmas Carol*

Many Christmases ago, I went to buy a doll for my son. I reached for the last one they had, but so did another man. As I rained blows upon him, I realized there had to be another way.

—MR. COSTANZA, from *Seinfeld*

Don't expect too much of Christmas Day. You can't crowd into it any arrears of unselfishness and kindliness that may have accrued during the past twelve months.

—OREN ARNOLD

A perfectly managed Christmas, correct in every detail is, like basted inside seams and letters answered by return, a sure sign of someone who hasn't enough to do.

—KATHARINE WHITEHORN

The threat of Christmas hung in the air, visible already in the fretful look of passersby as they readied themselves for the meaningless but necessary rites of false jovialities and ill-considered gifts.

—PETER DICKINSON, *Play Dead*

Christmas is a season of such infinite labour, as well as expense in the shopping and present-making line, that almost every woman I know is good for nothing in purse and person for a month afterwards, done up physically, and broken down financially.

—FANNY KEMBLE, British actor

I hear that in many places something has happened to Christmas; that it is changing from a time of merriment and carefree gaiety to a holiday which is filled with tedium; that many people dread the day, and the obligation to give Christmas presents is a nightmare to weary, bored souls; that the children of enlightened parents no longer believe in Santa Claus; that all in all, the effort to be happy and have pleasure makes many honest hearts grow dark with despair instead of beaming with goodwill and cheerfulness.

—JULIA PETERKIN, *A Plantation Christmas*

"Christmas won't be Christmas without any presents," grumbled Jo, lying on the rug.

—LOUISA MAY ALCOTT, *Little Women*

There are some people who want to throw their arms round you simply because it is Christmas; there are other people who want to strangle you simply because it is Christmas.

—ROBERT LYND, "On Christmas"

A Christmas shopper's complaint is one of long-standing.

—ANONYMOUS

"Attacked by Christmas toys. That's strange, that's the second toy complaint we've had."

—POLICE OFFICER,
from *The Nightmare Before Christmas*, 1993

Then God spoke to me and said:
People say only good things about Christmas.
If they want to say something bad,
they whisper.

—ANNE SEXTON,
"The Author of the Jesus Papers Speaks"

"Now I have a machine gun. Ho ho ho."

—HANS GRUBER (reading John McClane's note),
Die Hard, 1988

Another day, another million dollars.

—RICHARD DONAT, store manager,
Marshall Field and Co., Chicago

CINDY LOU WHO: "Santa, what's the meaning
of Christmas?"
GRINCH: "VENGEANCE! I mean...presents,
I suppose."

—*How the Grinch Stole Christmas*, 2000

Up, called up by drums and trumpets; these things and boxes having cost me much money this Christmas already, and will do more.

—SAMUEL PEPYS

So, I'm gettin' nuttin' for Christmas
Mommy and Daddy are mad.
I'm gettin' nuttin' for Christmas
'Cause I ain't been nuttin' but bad.

—S. TEPPER AND R. BENNETT, "Nuttin' for Christmas"

He who has no Christmas in his heart will never find Christmas under a tree.

—*Sunshine Magazine*

The hatred of "wanton Bacchanallian Christmases" spent throughout England...in "revelling, dicing, carding, masking, mumming, consumed in compotations, in interludes, in excess of wine, in mad mirth," was the natural reaction...against the excesses of a festival...dominated by a lord of misrule who did not hesitate to invade the churches in time of service, in his noisy revels and sports.

—ALICE MORSE EARLE,
"Customs and Fashions in Old New England"

Ho Ho Ho

In the old days, it was not called the Holiday Season; the Christians called it "Christmas" and went to church; the Jews called it "Hanukkah" and went to synagogue; the atheists went to parties and drank. People passing each other on the street would say "Merry Christmas!" or "Happy Hanukkah!" or (to the atheists) "Look out for the wall!"

—DAVE BARRY,
"Christmas Shopping: A Survivor's Guide"

Christmas is a time when everybody wants his past forgotten and his present remembered. What I don't like about office Christmas parties is looking for a job the next day.

—PHYLLIS DILLER

The Supreme Court has ruled that they cannot have a Nativity scene in Washington, D.C. This wasn't for any religious reasons. They couldn't find three wise men and a virgin.

—JAY LENO

Christmas at my house is always at least six or seven times more pleasant than anywhere else. We start drinking early. And while everyone else is seeing only one Santa Claus, we'll be seeing six or seven.

—W. C. FIELDS

One Christmas our dog, Vandi, stole The Baby Jesus from the Nativity scene, and my mother ran through the neighborhood in her housecoat screaming "Vandi, you eat that Baby Jesus you're going to doggy hell."

—ANNIE, from the television show
Caroline in the City

BETHANY: "Is your house on fire, Clark?"
CLARK GRISWOLD: "No, Aunt Bethany, those are the Christmas lights."

—From the movie *Christmas Vacation*, 1989

How does it happen that people with normal IQs and/or people who own a mirror, voluntarily walk out of the house wearing green and red sweaters with little embroidered Christmas trees and flashing-red-nosed-reindeer earrings?

—AMY KROUSE ROSENTHAL, *The Book of Eleven*

Well, I think we should get some bricks and some baseball bats and go over there and teach them the *true* meaning of Christmas.

—BERNICE, from the television show
Designing Women

Christmas begins about the first of December with an office party and ends when you finally realize what you spent, around April fifteenth of the next year.

—P. J. O'ROURKE

Aren't we forgetting the true meaning of Christmas? You know, the birth of Santa.

—BART SIMPSON, from *The Simpsons*

We celebrate the birth of one who told us to give everything to the poor by giving each other motorized tie racks.

—BILL MCKIBBEN

Please to put a nickel,
Please to put a dime.
How petitions trickle
In at Christmastime!

—PHYLLIS MCGINLEY, "Dear Madam:
We Know You Will Want to Contribute...,"

Roses are reddish. Violets are bluish. If it weren't for Christmas, we'd all be Jewish.

—BENNY HILL

A lovely thing about Christmas is that it's compulsory, like a thunderstorm, and we all go through it together.

—GARRISON KEILLOR, "Exiles"

Christmas is a strange season. We sing songs in front of dead trees and eat candy out of our socks.

—JOHN WAGNER, humorist

Be sure to mail your packages early so the post office can lose them in time for Christmas.

—Johnny Carson

Santa is very jolly because he knows where all the bad girls live.

—Dennis Miller

I did not know she'd take it so,
Or else I'd never dared:
Although the bliss was worth the blow,
I did not know she'd take it so.

—Countee Cullen, "Under the Mistletoe"

Wishes

I do hope your Christmas has had a little touch of eternity in among the rush and pitter patter and all. It always seems such a mixing of this world and the next—but that, after all, is the idea!

—EVELYN UNDERHILL, theologian

Thus, forgetting tricks and play
For a moment, Lady dear,
We would wish you, if we may,
Merry Christmas, glad New Year!

—LEWIS CARROLL, "Christmas-Greetings
(from a Fairy to a Child)"

God rest you merry, Innocents,
While Innocence endures.
A sweeter Christmas than we to ours
May you bequeath to yours.

—OGDEN NASH, "A Carol for Children"

I wish I could make merry Christmases as these
good people do, and be loved and thankful as
they are...

—LOUISA MAY ALCOTT,
"A Christmas Dream, and How It Came True"

I'm wishing at this Christmastime that I could
    but repay
A portion of the gladness that you've strewn
    along my way.

—EDGAR A. GUEST, "A Friend's Greeting"

May you have the gladness of Christmas which
    is hope;
The spirit of Christmas which is peace;
The heart of Christmas which is love.

—ADA V. HENDRICKS

At Christmas I no more desire a rose
Than wish a snow in May's new-fangled shows,
But like of each thing that in season grows.

—WILLIAM SHAKESPEARE, *Love's Labour's Lost*

I've just one wish
On this Christmas Eve
I wish I were with you.

—RICHARD CARPENTER AND FRANK POOLER,
    "Merry Christmas Darling"

Spirit

Christmas is not a time nor a season, but a state of mind. To cherish peace and goodwill, to be plenteous in mercy, is to have the real spirit of Christmas.

—CALVIN COOLIDGE

Over these tired, lonely, old faces had swept the transforming spirit of Christmas—a spirit that never pales, never ages, never loses its power.

—FLORENCE MAUTHE, "A Lonely Cafeteria"

Nearer and closer to our hearts be the Christmas spirit, which is the spirit of active usefulness, perseverance, cheerful discharge of duty, kindness and forbearance!

—CHARLES DICKENS,
"What Christmas Is As We Grow Older"

She felt uplifted by a great surge of wonder and gratitude and compassion and love. And she knew what it was. It was the spirit of Christmas. And it was upon them all.

—ARTHUR GORDON, "The Miraculous Staircase"

By trying to give away love, she brought the true spirit of Christmas into our lives, the spirit of selfless giving.

—NORMAN VINCENT PEALE, "A Gift of the Heart"

For the spirit of Christmas fulfils the greatest hunger of mankind.

—LORING A. SCHULER, author

As we struggle with shopping lists and invitations, compounded by December's bad weather, it is good to be reminded that there are people in our lives who are worth this aggravation, and people to whom we are worth the same.

—DONALD E. WESTLAKE

Christmas is not just a day, an event to be observed and speedily forgotten. It is a spirit which should permeate every part of our lives.

—WILLIAM PARKS, *Missions*

I wish we could put some of the Christmas spirit in jars and open a jar of it every month.

—HARLAN MILLER, author

For many of us, sadly, the spirit of Christmas is "hurry." And yet, eventually, the hour comes when the rushing ends and the race against the calendar mercifully comes to a close. It is only now perhaps that we truly recognize the spirit of Christmas. It is not a matter of days or weeks, but of centuries—nearly twenty of them now since that holy night in Bethlehem. Regarded in this manner, the pre-Christmas rush may do us greater service than we realize. With all its temporal confusion, it may just help us to see that by contrast, Christmas itself is eternal.

—BURTON HILLIS

Now, the essence, the very spirit of Christmas is that we first make believe a thing is so, and lo, it presently turns out to be so.

—STEPHEN LEACOCK, humorist and educator

"Look, Daddy! Teacher says every time a bell rings an angel gets his wings."

—Zuzu, from *It's a Wonderful Life,* 1946

Whatever else be lost among the years,
Let us keep Christmas still a shining thing.

—Grace Noll Crowell, "Let Us Keep Christmas"

It was always said of him, that he knew how to keep Christmas well, if any man alive possessed the knowledge. May that be truly said of us, and all of us! And so, as Tiny Tim observed, "God Bless Us, Every One!"

—Charles Dickens